MOTH

Southern Messenger Poets / *Dave Smith, Series Editor*

JANE SPRINGER

MOTH

poems

LOUISIANA STATE UNIVERSITY PRESS BATON ROUGE

Published by Louisiana State University Press
Copyright © 2018 by Jane Springer
All rights reserved
Manufactured in the United States of America
LSU Press Paperback Original
First printing

Designer: Michelle A. Neustrom
Typeface: Miller Text

Library of Congress Cataloging-in-Publication Data

Names: Springer, Jane, 1969– author.
Title: Moth : poems / Jane Springer.
Description: Baton Rouge : Louisiana State University Press, [2018]
Identifiers: LCCN 2017059767| ISBN 978-0-8071-6792-2 (softcover :
  acid-free paper) | ISBN 978-0-8071-6793-9 (pdf) | ISBN 978-0-8071-
  6794-6 (epub)
Classification: LCC PS3619.P757 A6 2018 | DDC 811/.6—dc23
LC record available at https://lccn.loc.gov/2017059767

CONTENTS

MOTH

Whooo Whooo

O life little life little sawdust speck in the eye of the universe—blind I tried
to tie these days with string & print where fang & claw are cracked
little cups, a notebook jarred with specimens winged-done then
shrunk in basement smoke, the jail I thought I just
deserved—while wind's cheek turned to what
flew, I could not flown—little truck
I drove instead of run, little
life—above the ruins,
the owl, my son.

The Ghost, the Driver, the Martyr

Then the ghost sent a great wind through the corn & such a violent storm arose
the tractors threatened to overheat.

All the drivers were afraid & each cried out to his own granary. & they threw
personal radios to the field path to lighten the load.

But the martyr stayed in the root cellar, where she lay down in Dreamlandia.

Not even coyotes could wake her: 'How can you sleep? Get up and call on your
DJ to restore productivity.'

Then the drivers said to each other, 'Come, let us paper scissors rock
to determine who is responsible for this cataclysm.'

& it was all scissors to the martyr's paper. So they asked her, 'Tell us, who's
to blame for heisting our livelihood? What kind of work do you do?

What realm do you dwell in? Who are your
people? What's the zip?'

She said, 'I am worshipper of the last native tree whose roots poison the soil &
whose fruits fall on the witless squirrel yet

when the green husks ferment several months, issues forth an indelible ink—
even if my peeps once were blue skinks & from the map of my marker

comes barks so various they never repeat.'

Salt Map

I'm searching for the warehouse of beaches where Archimedes counts sand
I've got a problem with the counting, not the math—but the money
in the moneychanger's hand & the smokestack, not the oxygen, the fire
in the nostril of an ass—but the jukebox in the warehouse where
the counting goes down rolls under the siren's wave-
leveled shotguns, wake of new construction, clamshack
where you couldn't find an accidental pearl if you led all the buffalo
from auction to the ocean—& wouldn't that add up to another wrong
junction? It used to be

on Gains St. where the wild orange ranged—I'm looking for the stingray
in a gravel parking lot, sea oats sweeping busted windows, not the
glass—but some translucence & I get so tired of propaganda: Eat More
Seaweed! It's misleading—a teensy-weensy sphere eluding grasp, stuck
to wings of no-see-ums, swatting, losing, not the Fuji or
figgy pudding—but the sunburn peeling back to original skin
& it's taken seven days to get the salt map with its axis of symmetry
aligned, I've a problem with the logic, not the beaches—but the cosmic
sale that came, beforehand.

Letter from the North Country

Dear Southland,

We arrived safe—how could we not? With every dirtroad pillowed asphalt & the
picnic-fields: Tabled, raked Zen? Where blazed wild fire-flower, grew steel signs:

Don't Touch Them.

& even if we wanted, we could not get lost. Picture spot: Target painted where
to pose on a precipice boulder.

                    Slate shards rained south from mountain shoulder.

If we'd wanted to get tangled up in teasel & go rolling lawless? Fenced
pasture. Fixed paths
spiked the trailhead
forever looping back
on where we started.

                    Why search the northside of spruce for moss?

Goodbye, rose-fingered
           eastern dawn & cowhand sun
                  settling west—
                          compass relics: Southern
                                Cross & old Polaris.

Mile markers measured probable exhaustion—we rested in the shelter designated
for rain & remained dry as sand in the trachea while downpour made a gulf

in our lungs. & being so cared for, I forget how to resuscitate, to cinch
the tourniquet—canna lily, saw palm. Is there such a thing as too safe? We were glad

to find no rattlesnakes & pitched the hatchet.

Do Not Cut Browse for Bed—who does that anymore? Don't Carve Your Heart
in the Beech—why carry a knife? No signs

of wildlife—as if raccoons lay tased in chickenwire cages bound for elsewhere.

Had bear made mischief?
                              Blood growl, chalk outline.

& I thought of you—Don't Jump, Don't Swim. Watching Chittenango Falls
fall behind a chainlink fence—

how nearly we gashed our feet on your shored cans—yet skinnydipping
your blue sinkholes, we

            wafted down from daylight

        into buoyant

            bodies,

                3 Wakulla angels

            lighting

                on strangers' roofs.

Gulf

Somewhere in the mountains is a Gulf sells: Chargers, rhinestone
lighters, trucker's speed, & cowhide keyrings, pinespray,
bugwipes, sheepsgut, pizza, earplugs, pigears, ass
wipes, & camo-condoms, toy guns, ciggies, ice
bags, horselips, stickers, blackcats, jesus
bracelets, cameras, eagle sweatbands,
postcards, aspirin, permits, & organic
pumpkin seeds. The clerk behind
the counter's old as: Walking 40
miles to work, sci-fi stations,
Burma shave ads, up by boot
straps, Jello salad tossed w/
hot dogs, silk socks, board-
ing house gazettes, pinochle,
lobotomies, & washboards,
Jim crow, petting parties,
stealing melons, sneezing
wheat pennies into white
handkerchiefs. Screwed
to his checkout is a new
touchscreen with boxes,
so patrons weigh-in real-
time, e.g.: Does this clerk
smile, clean up good? &
does he ask if you need
add-ons: 'NASCAR cap, miss?
KY jelly?' Does he slap you
five, or fist bump: 'Thanks for
coming'—does he otherwise
solicit interest in his cock ring?

He's Bangladeshi-Queens-
Jamaican accent, graying,
hip hurts where he
soldiered grand
kids, needs swing
shift, fry cook,
starched jeans—
which reminds me,

let's play a game: We're cousins. You get drunk,
sleep in my bathtub, we'll make out. Let's play
Amish. We'll hoe tomatoes, if they die you're
fired. Ok, now you're bossman. I get 5 bucks
if I wear a mop wig, but I have to lick the
toilets if I can't turn profit singing the
'Bad Boys' cop song in piglatin every
time a customer says 'Howdy.'

Let's play in the Gulf
between the artificial
& the genuine:

Have I stood straight
for this portrait, have
I let my real self like
a seal turn supple in
the Disney pool of:
May I kiss your pretty
cufflinks? Have I sparkled
for as little as is possible to pay
me—do I tattoo, bleach my own
roots, don't you motocross to see me
in this zoo as if I'll piss into the register if
you're not there to urge me, gently, not to? The gulf

is such between us, watched & watching—

let's play gracious: Sakes Alive.

Let's play felon—

Rate Me.

Winter Reading

Once an 1800's Adirondack camp guide spent 2 glorious pages explaining
to me his joy at walking many towns' distance in search of the head he'd
shape into an axe blade—material mattered, be it steel or nickel. I was so
new to the region I recognized only 3 trees in his path: Oak, redbud,
maple—& he spent the next page elaborating benefits of each fresh-
grained handle.

I read him the year after this gal down home dared me lift my T, then
licked my nipple.

He sojourned upriver, encountering swarms of winged, flesh-eating pests
that make mosquitoes from southern climes seem songbirds. He boiled
a salve to soothe his whelps & wrapped all but his eyes in a kerchief
continuing, undeterred, while listing medicinal ingredients—a woodsman's
mantra of natural opiates. In tone, he gloated.

The bar'd been littered with blooms, I was loaded.

By the time night fell he was well in the woods, having passed a Penobscot
Camp, he bemused how mothers tied their infants to boards leaned against
trees. This custom didn't seem so strange to me, as you could tan three deer
in the time it takes to entertain one milk-thirsty yowler otherwise left free
to teethe a batch of poison arrows—but I gather the guide, having none
of his own kids, was full of vigor.

The darer's tongue brushed me sable as an artist's rigger & we went home
with viewers.

His most exalted passage derived from fire of others, as with rueful wit he
recalled reckless young loggers would set a mansion's worth of wood aflame
to ruin their suppers in one 40 foot blaze of cracked mash bottles & song,
then wake damp in their clothes without a stick of lumber to weather the
morning frost, while he could cook for himself a week & keep dry on three
bars of well-placed timber.

If I owned an axe back then, I don't remember.

While he plodded with the swiftness of one attempting bare-handed
fishing, oiling his hat or darning socks on a rock, red tailed hawks
made come-cries overhead. He spent dusk whacking out a lean-to's
haven from wind & feathering a brush bed like a Zen master. Before
sleep he'd don a muslin gown & catalogue the day's wild tubers.

I do remember waking to well-pantied lawn, boots in kitchen, friends,
W.B. spooning my dog, & taking orders: Who wants eggs, turnovers?

Centuries passed, it seemed, lakes froze around him in his holy macho ode
to suffering. I couldn't find the handle for his pine & pitch in surrender of salt,
solitudinous ardor over caught, charred rabbit, wisdom-smizdom—albeit
wooded, not *so* unlike Virgil proselytizing *Eclogues* in pastures of cooked-up
shepherds hell bent on shearing full estates of sheep free of their wool—

ergo alter-mate to his unread conclusion:

> Come over now? Naked women, devil music.

Velvetleaf

Tick of sweet clover, swinecress parasite, did you have a music
made you stick to the first warm alien who swung our old
scythe through your brome? Our Boy wanting to better scope
the renegade deer & private fox, your creekside tinderbox—
shored up cricket space, puncturevine hiding place—how did
velvetleaf become home worth leaving, Tick of time, of Lyme
design—had you neither thee, nor thine to keep you pining,

but had to claim mine?

& Tick of brine stuck in your jelly wound, insidious, now you're
buried inside a dissolvable body—don't you mind? Can blood
be ambrosial as what wine you drank by driftwood—each
night's watery bell choir of coyotes had to ring better than
listening to Queen stuck on repeat in our son's bedroom,
dog hair tumbleweeds, Comics heaped bedsheets—you might
have jetted eagle's breast, instead, or drummed nectar

in honeysuckle's ear

with your own tick-mate to call you dear.

One Late Bee

& bullseyed belly Boy, struck: Isn't New York one long yell
of shady contracts writ on fleabane? How I love your winglet,
atrophied 3 months, limp club flung towards the Zombie
Apocalypse—you kick ground-guts barefoot in the same
weeds of the crimescene where you got tick-shot, walnuts
bomb the tin shed, you want to make whole hosts of
dead we can't see gnashing to eat our brains, more dead?

Me too.

Me wish you don a poison vest, gluey song for death pests,
shouldn't we veil you in Deet & teach you to hold a sword
in your teeth? Shouldn't we strip you for a body check
each time you waltz indoors, soak you in bleach? But
what is there to do but let you keep swinging away
from childhood—oblivious to the next symptom of how
we fail to keep you safe from harm's bastard pin-prick?

Lilac leaves stay green in a winter who refuses to come,

even as I write this—
outdoors, watching you,
wanting a hymn to
turn the other cheek
or love recluse equal
to vulture by the time
I get to the end, for
you, for us—one late
bee bitters me, honey
I don't want, anaphylactic
dodge & swat,
gestures not good as
the Buddha-esque mood
I wanted for you—
to be zooless yet meek
as a stuffed unicorn—
if you got only one life
lord, would you have
been a proper mother
& hexed the world to
have your sacrifice back?

Paper

Damned if I'll be the woman who collects mass produced throw pillows counts
her county's condoms shoots chemicals to drench the porch
hornet on the way to recycle the obits hums Somalian
rap—young—five minutes till the end one spring
considers the GPS tracking in relation to the
real cost of cell surveillance buys a hand
gun walks the dog dips Fritos in peanut
butter Googles Selfie! sixteen ways
from Sunday.

        There are two kinds
of origami: The one kind is a dragon
with 1000 scales cut so intricately wings
flap unfolding—this takes hours of exact labor
it takes a cliff's cave of jewels, lace you'd commit hara-
kiri for to see or touch again. The other kind's a gentle bend
in the plain paper tower's middle makes me cry, I won't be that woman

either—sifting strangers' receipts from the ashes of downed town silos
to say whose fault is this move to the new age
of Victorian? Whose fist clutches
shifting sand? Nor plunder
coins to match
the old beloved's eyes that
wander fresh possibility—being
no mechanical & flag wrapped patriot of one
country, but swear allegiance to margin's error, headline: Careful, Concrete

Crushed by Falling Sheet Where the Greedy Surrender to New Foliage.

Swallow

In the gulf between us sinks a parish of Sherman's burned plantations
& the hoary school of no books, Sex Ed, Foreign Language,

no Music or Art, Math taught only odd years, we never get to square
root, records say that's fault of white flight driving our peers to

private quarters when integration longbows past the town of Newellton.
In Upstate NY they're villages—towns, where the school board

votes in new auditoriums, Olympic pools to serve public good. I'd like
to thank Mr. Prince for whirling a winged eraser upside our heads,

for passing notes that said 'T stirs the best fuzzy navels, but
Avondree eclipses his strut,' as erasure renders portraiture more

clear: It's Bob Burns' family who blasts illegal DDT from crops
to gullet to dead birds flanking flyspeck highways, they own all

tillable land, we can rent it, or work it for wages of Mexican migrants,
whose kids stomp cotton while Future Farmers of America serves

as class to cancel Spanish & we suffer essays on the best speed limit
to 'Stay Alive, Drive 55.' The pearled librarian from my

new Upstate locale pokes fun at this trivia: 'Well *Louisiana*, you can
understand'—& you can! You get the distinction continually

drilled in here: North as worthy, South as punishment—the way you
get why not to mix Crown Royal w/ 2 dollar wine, or how by

detasseling corn too far down the stalk you get a fistful of spikes. It's
an unforgiving 99 degrees & no AC in a hotbox we're so used to

we don't bother wasting money on the . . . joules? it takes to turn fans
or replace the faltering façade, foundation, roof over Newellton

High School, XZY school on the scale of students deserving address.
Thank you, Mrs. Frazier, for teaching how to etherize frogs &

keep them pinned while scalpel-ing, dissections teach us to poke our
subjects gently—as in the gulf between us exists 21 distinct

grouper species, classes dwindled as our downstate uncles fishing the
coming omen of oilspills & aunts, suspended on premonition's

bridge—a hurricane, though we don't know the name yet for babes
tossed to the Gulf's arms, rocked in the salt waves, the song

sargassum makes feathering them, waked, changed. Thanks, Mrs. Hall,
for 'Thanatopsis,' from the *Yale Book of American Verse:*

> '. . . . . When thoughts
> Of the last bitter hour come like a blight
> Over thy spirit, and sad images
> Of the stern agony, and shroud, and pall,
> And breathless darkness, and the narrow house,
> Make thee to shudder, and grow sick at heart;'—

as though you knew the sum of us who fleshed out family income in
dank woodland trailers of prostitution, then wore white for

baptismal coronations in Lake Bruin where cottonmouth is governor
& mosquito, state bird—all information left off standard

college tests, along with how to season possum & which neighbors
served the KKK—what bayou was it? Where the lynched

of our town's othered loved ones gingered waters, catfish fluttering
rib cages in our version of myth which the *Princeton Guide*

to Poetry & Poetics tells me archeologists just discovered stories bury
truth: 6 Troys existed in the columns fused with sediment.

How deep is the gulf between us? How deep can a Louisiana teen,
whether glowing ember/walnut/white as Dixie plate, fathom

the river-deep beard of Massachusetts-bred, accentual syllabic bent,
cupid of the funeralesque, William Cullen Bryant who suggests

'Thou go not, like the quarry-slave at night,
Scourged to his dungeon, but, sustained and soothed
By an unfaltering trust . . .'

when nowhere in our Civics class yields terms for Washington C's
wealth of peanuts, Anne Frank, Japanese internment camps,

let alone L'Ouverture's Revolution—the gulf is deep as outer space
where you can *tsk tsk* 'just desserts' wrought upon the heads of

children's chillren's, chirrun of overseers & slaves while praising facts:
Your kind won't breach this galaxy, 'that's how deep' the joke

ends. Yet, in Upstate NY it's 'Happy Chinksgiving' according to the
HS hockey team, they've spelled it out in noodles, sweet sauce

cross the walls of the China Sea & toss hot mustard at the girls who
try pushing doors in on their lunchbreak, troubling gulf waters

where they shallow, lap the shoreline—sometimes it's only sand
between us. I say 'you' but mean 'us' though we've never shared a

class, the gulf so deep you have to ask 'is that your *real* accent' or
roll your eyes *How twee* when I mix up the Kabbalah with the

Torah (isn't overcoming all the gaps in rural class exhausting?)—
reminds me of the principal of Newellton High School measuring

our shorts short-fall with his own reptilian hands before ordering
us home, a 'No Excuses' mantra extended to the ceremony

of senior bequeathals to us juniors: To David Merritt, we leave a
school bus to carry Jane's bodacious tatas, & a butt!

Well, not everything we should have is what we ended with in the
gulf between us, the levee's not firm as that, sand boils can't

keep from boiling up, we're worried, we are drowning, we are not
the ones voting, or bailing out from war or peace, we are

writing to *you* all the time,
I am *writing.* with *both hands, day and night.*

What is love? The 2 five year olds at the adjacent Elementary must
be asking before the superintendent issues them a year long's

suspension for dropping their
pants & trying how to *do it*

on a shared nap mat—

was that punishment enough? I want to ask, with a NY toll taker's
bitchiness, or nuance of the well-bred, but I can't because I

left Newellton, too, Thrace of Philomenas' cut-out tongues, where
the school is boarded up between us in the weeds' decadent

tapestry.

Pink

Just how cold is it? Cold as a flamingo lodged
headfirst in snowdrift after the trucker
marauded its flock, poisoned its
mom, jacked it, cereal number &
tagged then clipped it, so it
kerplunked a 70's wood-
beaded seat instead of
winging out the cab,
replete w/carotenoid
snacks engineered
to preserve this
bird's pink as
brine shrimp
used to suit
outside his one

flamingo zoo—
what he didn't
guess, this god
of the eighteen-
wheeler, is the bird
knew campy songs
out the wazoo, from
'3 Chartreuse Buzzards' to
Kum Ba Yah, which she
sang w/Fruitloops spilling
her shallow-keeled mandible
for thousands of tundra-miles—
flapping down & up the wipers &
flipping off his hat by bill to keep beat,
that's how cold it was—& curiously satisfying.

Calling Home

When you said Goodbye, stranger, I thought you meant the Leon Pub juke
box where Major Tom got stuck that night & ground control was just
the bitch waitress who checked our age for kicks then sped our longnecks
down the bar as if she'd like to wreck us, permanent, on Blondie's Mars—

    not this golden capped
  fruit bat, inquisitive
in upside down, his smile
a frown.

Maybe you meant the Dancing queen in Al Green's church of Won't you
help me, girl? *I'm sorry I didn't shoo the pest you said shared collective
consciousness from the ceiling teetering your bed—but made you come party,
instead, for all I didn't do you did for me—*

      & not this red-handed
      howler monkey orange flame flaring
      through the trees we may not
      see again?

Between the darts of Leon Pub, the Weather Girls predicted raining men—
thank you for deluging me the Pet Shop Boys to *Summerteeth* & Beck defying
speed of loneliness, we wore diamond footsoles, didn't we? Earth below us,
drifting, falling, floating

     armored pangolin
     whose perfect rolling
    form once outplayed the wit
    of predators.

I surely did enjoy my stay, before you Goodbyed Mary, Jane & mostly think
Let it be—the splif, the joint, & blunt, if time could keep Anne Murray's waltz
jammed up between two pool tables where we could have this dance at 28,
eternally, a leather patched elbow blast—

Goodbye stranger must have meant some future date where Some they do &
some they don't survive the Desperado days, the Pancho Lefty left, & too
fast Little red corvette where You send me. Darlin you do, you do! We don't
accrue them back—

black shoe which I have lived as a

> Monte Iberia Eluth,
> centimetering bright racing
> stripes while shrilling
> forest's thrill—

Then too, Let it bleed surely didn't mean let's go poach rhinos, elephants, Good
bye stranger, it's been nice?

O my love is a Craklin rose
O my love is a Raspberry hat
O my love is a critical list
of endangered relations with this—

> bubal hartebeest
> of wavish horn waving
> time past rock-savvy
> hoof,

past orbit, stabilizers up, running perfect, starting to collect requested data,
what will it effect, thou sweet cliché of appointments, agents, movie scripts,
I hope you find your paradise—but We are family & this my plea *per condition
#3 of our Mutual Contract of Destruction:*

How many poems
must I write you
before you
send me
the new CD
you've owed me since I
i-tuned you that last soul song come *on* you can't tell me it didn't get to you.

Gasoline Psalm

O bird bird bird are you lonely tonight, in the branches emptied of other
bird feet, where silence creaks in the woods' deep swing—

am I such a gaudy billboard with a luger promising: '20 to Life,'
you won't land on me?

Am I a toy cab junk-heaped on the tacky lawn you passed, sunflowers
bloomed in adjacent fields this afternoon.

Tired bird I hear but don't see, the bourbon licked wing of churches
where daddy preached, a psalms thrall

warped in the wire of me,

what I could confess tonight—it would take 3 Jesuses to wear out the
cross of me, where you dived & eddied,

I contracted & lodged, robbed Peter, paid Paul, got gasoline, having
none to feed, cried over a plain pecan—

but I would bury my own talon to grow you a tree of birds right now,
trash talkers in curlers & the soup pot on.

Moth

I should stop smoking. For in my body, the world's largest moth
closes her wings over Georgia, U-pick tomato fields,
red ripe plump lungs I had back then, dew wet, pungent, we can't
all be tough fruit, juicy—I miss mowing fields there in a bikini
across the dirt road from the Mexican farmer, soaked
bandana holding his hair back, gloss winged crow, we breathed
so easy, working our rows, neither waving nor speaking—
the sky grew lungs there—crepe myrtle budding.

Her giant cloud wings storm out the Gulf shore—submerge boats,
so down with dreams I could have been a Florida sailor
hauling up oysters, water licked pearl lungs I had then,
enough fresh air to swim out past Dog Island, instead of these
coughing up salt lungs, we can't all be so glistening—
I miss combing the beach at night where turtles lugged
suitcase bodies through sea oats, breathing was easy—even
the sunset had great lungs there, pink & spongy.

Some days her wings unhinge, joggers pass on their way to yoga,
I moved to the Adirondacks' feet, you have to hide your
moth here, where health is Zion, I snuff my cigarettes in a pocket
& shut my mouth to keep my moth from flying out—this is not
Alabama, you can't pick up a nice hitchhiker, smoke over
waffles in a truck stop, find a blues dive to singe the wings
of the moth winging in your ribcage—in Alabama,
lungs echoed in trumpets, ditto sad dobros.

Some days I forget I hold two cigarettes feeding two moth wings
simultaneously, they gain weight, press so hard I barely
make out docks by Pontchartrain—it's not that I want to paddle
back through swampland where my lungs inhaled & exed wild
iris, I know Louisiana moss was fat with redbugs, pollen
puffed asthmatic halos, cottonmouth always killing some kid
who drug his stick in the wrong muck, where any lung
with two legs, somehow, got screwed up.

If you said, in Mississippi, *My moth eats a hole in the wool of my breath*
they'd think you're drunk, all lungs are tank tops, cottony,
humid—I miss cattle egret, guess those fields were a 7-11 serving
Big Gulps of mosquitoes, how, you ask, could I miss the South
so much a moth makes dust rags from my insides? Or, if you
loved it, why then leave it? Maybe I didn't—but I ran so fast there
trains seemed lazy, even sitting still for Sunday football, my
lungs rode high on wind between quarterbacks.

What is my moth—I ask the lord. If I move back home will she
dissolve—in the region where my ex-lovers leave a trail
of tears to Texas & mother's ashes make an acid soil for magnolia
to grow in? I miss my sister & daddy hoeing up lungs there—
my friend in his small green house, pouring bourbon
to beat back his own moth—is she death I am half in love
with? One wing caved black from loss, the other a tourniquet
to save heart-sap from leaking down porch steps?

The only distinction between a moth & a butterfly is clubbed
antennae. It is January, white moths fall from the clouds
outside my body—I should put on skis & flatten them cross-
country like everyone else in the Adirondack foothills, where
my feet are clubs, where my moth folds over old
geography I should stop burning, like houses here burn with
their families still in them—I should learn to love, or want
lungs opening like two giant, born-again peonies.

Buffalo Escape Gem Family Farm, Get Shot

Herd of Upstate buffalo finds glitch in the fence one afternoon—just
like this April not to snow, not to keep long waves of purple phlox
from blooming by the hogweed that blinds those trying to gather it
into a bouquet, we're a runaway meat train galloping the pasture
between ditches with our kin in tow, out of our own dung ranging
new meadowfood, nasturtium, dandelion leaves—worshiping sun &
shade, slow grade of hills rolling rock to hooves, it feels so good to
flush a lark-flock skyward into hoopla, they thought they had us

bolted up, 'cute humps!' I may have said myself, driving past them,
'complacent as a cows' or 'sad' before the glitch got seen—a meanness
I didn't mean, & in the vast imagination I go with them as if they
could trample my captors' fence, too, we plunge the Hudson not
believing we could swim before this 3 mile river width, it feels
so good to tread against containment, weightless, go wherever—
good to shiver in new temperature, wet/cold current shocking
us alive to shoulder what never was shank—hope is the hemlock

scent rising from the opposite bank—trees un-felled by emerald
beetles, a thicket of bees sounding orange trumpetvine we recall
memories so deep, we know without asking not to bother them, not
to mess with the timber rattlesnake's bluestone shelter, loose animals
are dangerous the billboards flanking highway 87 read us, we do not
read them—there's too little time with riflemen kneeling at the guard
rail above us in traffic slowed to halt, for northern metalmark, columbine
dusky wings flutter by, we, who've not yet rolled in chicory, with our one

calf, fleeing Bethlehem NY, too little time for sinking into Onesquethaw
Creek where the water rushes garnet as wine it's our first time to drink.

Dear Eurydice,

You must have stood here. With the Cretan dwarf Megacerine grazing
the same fare where you got snakebit. We know it was not tame
there, warriors hurtled sand boas on board your Grecian gold
fleece-seeking ships to cause chaos. What odd javelins the
snakes made—defanged not to poison your own soldiers
yet capable of slithering limbs—it's not the snakes who
wrecked the isthmuses but common fear of otherness.

You must have thought the world's a wedding made for
singing before you got snakebit. Each squeak & chirp,
accompaniment—beside the asphodel, the wolf's
bane breaking open bells, before you fell down
death's dumb ears, you must have smelled the
lavender that grows wild on your island, still—
& felt perennial rain's vow. You did not stand

where I stand now, where acid floods the rain's
clean vow, we clone the chirps to mimic sames,
a band of blands that needs no blooming but for
medicine—with weddings done beside the chicken
plant, where we don masks to bear the shitty scent
of meat's raw coop, cacophony are pesticides sounding
the aphid, armyworm—rootworm, snake, & earworm mute.

Poor myth-gaffed snake. Who once confounded warring
Greeks & paralyzed their heroines—or coiffed the crown
of their revenge, or venomed suicidal queens, or cushioned
the thrones under them—how do you do our zoo's aquarium
removed of grasses' privacy, as patrons knock the day-long glass
requiring rapt attention, how do you like the hand that drops in mice—
instead of dragging your game down to better see, how brief, the range?

Eurydice, Do you possess a sense of humor? When we shoot a herd of buffalo
    here in Paradise, do you make room for them in Hades saying,
'Move over bacon, it's new meatier

bovine-things?' Do they pay permit for entry, do you clear the stairs of
    slaughters to make more slaughters fit, do you sue for damages
if one falling buffalo cracks your

head in? Or is Hades a 'Humans/Gods Only Space' as we designated
    heaven—so the buffalo just flap in buzzards' gullets for infinity?
What about Mohicans—with you,

do they famish for home-cooking, do the cows get eaten? Totemically,
    who's higher, T-Rex gets dibs or Genghis—is swordier or Holly-
wood teeth favored, or is it a women/children

first thing, what's leftover—
do you cut the hides
for stool your ruler
idles feet on? A wooly
cape he sweats in, skin
he drums regrets in—

or as you, do dead buffalo get new life, post-mortem, in what condition?
    Do you tag their ears & store each species separate cave—do
fresh buffalo mix with extinct antiquus

& occcidentalis inmates? How fine a point spears your distinctions, do
    you number each buffalo hair before deciding which chamber?
We've made such cages, here,

we've barbed the plains down to an acre, roofed the sky, & troughed
    the lakes for buffalo in paradise, we hardly ever meet them
strolling on their skeletons

outside their UPCs. It's not good for economy—buffalo stampeding
off commercial script, is it the idea of free buffalo I miss—

dangerous strangers

tumbling the lawn

to test our love of nature's

limitlessness?

Am I projecting too much animal grief onto you, Eurydice? I can't believe your
one fidelity was to one human, that's Virgil's version where your life's reduced to

wife. It's Virgil keeps you cast in hell, where elsewhere you're a vision sent
to punish Orpheus for ego. If not Hades, where but here do you reside, past life?

The century's myth that interests me is Alison Bechdel's—where women speak
to women past the macro-scopal galaxy of soldiering.

What would our
conversation be? Talk

to me.

Let's talk of art, from

damsel fly air-brushing jade
across fawn shade to water-

bug on silver skates &

underneath the lake's
translucent cornea—

protists too much
to name, who
gulp the sun's
light for be-
speckled trout
& bream bespeckling
soft sand-cratered beds
as strange as any Martian
cave. The slightest life
forms interest me.
The grackle seeming
oiled onyx feather-
spill until she lights in
light,
then hooded
azure down to
indigo—a jonquil
iris circles pools
that give her
subaqueous
sight.

On Finding the Lost Scissors

& there will be very little nudity except for the soft underbelly
of ibis jalapeños in the greens

you thought all the angels ate sorghum & drank Courvoisier?

& there will be primal tears in the shag carpet tea-olive
oscillating from the fan even now you are nodding

having accepted you'll never be home again.

Woo

O life little life little sawdust fleck I thought we'd go on riding hip-to-hip
   on the bench seat of Big Blue gassing up at Hoggly Woggly supping
    junk food & coke summers so hot cops slept with radars
    in their laps in the shadetree crook of Swamp Creek Rd the FM
   dialed past gospel to Led Zeppelin, Outcast, incandescent
from love of county glass flea-market bowl packed crypto blown
seeds out the crank window broke barns & that appaloosa
up to flanks in poppies pulling down side roads to lick-a me suck-a you—

Not this Boko Harem Hamas Komalah Jihad—Vanguard of Conquest
crouched in orobanche whispering *mother me*, tamarind & apricot
 crushed in our tire tracks, deluge so the wipers stuck
  trying to get the bullets off & refugees teaching us the notes of bazooki
   from the flatbed drones we don't know our asses from our
    camel shit hookah we gerryrigged the muffler with by accident
    & winter's brown body is the street sign in this desert where
      little life, you suggest we just keep all eyes on the road from now on?

Squeezebox

Mr. Bob says you can't get a free POW flag
 from the VFW he looked hither & yon,
  but Herb Phillipson's sells them for change—
& two holidays a year get you get a free
dinner at Applebee's even if you have to
pay for your wife, just that & tax, but
it's a nationwide chain & costs them a lot
of dead presidents probably millions for
 every Vet, no matter what war—he does
  not seem happy, he is crying on the lawn

  in the exact place yesterday's blue spar
   hawk held a goldfinch to the dirt in its
    talons accordion-style, really weird because
the finch made a joyful sound in death's
secret prison, *fuck that* mixed-up feeling
of wanting to record the common horror
while simultaneously scaring off the
hawk, who has to eat—& wanting to hold
 Mr. Bob somehow makes you the one with
  talons, as it's a private moment between you.

Wah Wah Pedal

& When a blues band shops for real music it may cost a walk, an hour or year,
a man left by a woman, a chest of guns—

two suns.

➤

So this longneck gets her own war. She can't believe the fireworks parading
through her chest.

Her table so changed:
The Army-issue breakfast—she pees real bullets.

She's happy, but there are times her apartment window combusts.

➤

Last night two sons of guns shoot bullets at an army of doves. But it's dark,
they miss—& a blues man becomes

a changed woman.

➤

So this man, a real firecracker, parades through the door holding an Iraqi
boy across his chest. Tells me he can't believe war

is good & puts the little boy to sleep with a shot of music. Who am I to tell
him what to do?

We make love with his gun, then breakfast.

➤

No combusted doves, here, or bullet breakfast—changed times left the Army
in a rock bar, happy.

The doves? Sometimes Eve lets them sleep beside her cheek.

➤

So this woman in a Little Rock bar walks up & tells me about her son she loves
who returned from Iraq 10 years ago today.

Two longnecks cost a dollar, it's Happy Hour.

She lets him sleep with his gun across his chest—who is she to tell him what
to do—he left a boy, now a man, the gun aids sleep.

Sometimes when making breakfast—she can't believe it's him at her table so
changed. He's ok but there are times.

Last New Year's Eve they made it through the afternoon parade, were window
shopping when firecrackers combusted & he dove

under a truck, would not come out. The time she got up in the dark to pee he
shot a bullet through the door beside her cheek.

How is she to tell him—time he get his own apartment?

They play good music in this bar, a real blues band.

The Rock

The coral in the mortar seems not to do with a second kiss behind
 the fortuneteller's booth, Spike Easterling's Bubblicious mouth parted,
  tectonic plates to admit hostages—we did not understand, that year
   Ali's proposal to my sis, eating kookoo sabzi & osh on pillows in our
    socks could be dangerous, braces caught—I thought Spike quartz to
     my feldspar, that Ayatollah was Khomeini's birth name, we thought
      plain water too severe for supper—at the fair, Spike's hand all day in
       my back pocket, lamb we pet then had to put back to get my sister's
        passport—I liked the new ziggurat scarf fluttered waves in her hair,
         Jimmy Carter's name conjured peanuts & the hall of mirrors where his
          brother stayed drunk enough to brand his own beer, there's a carnival
           incense floats over bleating commercials for uranium, *esfand*—reminds

            me of diabase, dactite—the rhyolite of Iran, less than all the bowing we
             did in Ali's apartment, prayer mats rolled up like magic carpets & ticket
              to the double Ferris wheel of my sister's almost-marriage, chador folded
               in her suitcase if suitcase served as temple, hard rock scrambled by the
                scrambler, cigarette butts smashed by cotton candy in the mudwash by
                 the fair gate, rock of ages, rock of oil lamps, olives, if only I hadn't kissed
                  Spike's brother, first, that morning's rollercoaster wrecked between two
                   possible countries—market lamb's full head on ice in the kitchen, Amy's
                    crying, failed Operation Eagle Claw—then Ali's eerie disappearance,
what love elects may appear glassy to aphanitic to porphyritic deception,
Rock, who first settled you in Cain's hand?

The Mamas

The hair pick's missing. Not your mama's, my mama's. Now her hair's going
to look a hot mess. She puts it in the same place. Did you take it? Admit
you did, adolescence cancels sense—where your brain once lolled there's
a laser tag mall. If you don't return it before she tangles we'll get mangled.
Hear That? She rifles for it in the make-up drawer—'Prelude to Hell for All's'
what that track's called, & it wouldn't make the playlist if you hadn't skipped
church. 'Can't I Have Anything I Own' is the next drone before you hit her
No Fly Zone. You want to be how the last fly looting sugar from her looks?

Must be you want the oranges-for-Christmas story—the rented fridge
I swear to god you had to drop a nickel in the door to open it for milk until
the thing got paid for & you've never even had to share a bed with your sister.

Not my mother, yours. Thinking cash buds from magnolias. No warpath,
no crusades, you waste paste on your toothbrush like you'll always get
more—as in heaven where wrists sprout plucky picks for hands & everybody
scores Godiva for din din because your mama's sweet hereafter don't have
repo men. You'd like that, admit it. Preferring not to think up what the mamas,
mad or holy, think. Meanwhile backwoods Louisiana people practice hygiene
by picking molars with twigs—no drillings—no fillings. Think I'm fibbing?
Google it. Whole families make do with one instrument for hair, they put picks

back in the forest where they found them, they share.

Stranger's Song

Blessed is the one who don't
do-si-do with the man
or vogue in the way that gunmen take
or sit in the company of harangues
but whose delight is in creek that has no face
& who meditates on its current day and night.
That metaphysical giant is like a stranger's song
which sidles the lawn
& whose barn does not weather
whatever they love becomes better than law.

Not so the others
they are like spammed ads
jellied in the can
therefore they can't stand in the awareness
or speculate in the choir of plain nature
for the Groove watches over the way of the devoted
but the way of the others leads yonder.

Lilacs

& in the gulf between us smokes Wagyu beef infused w/gold-leaf & fois
gras slapped w/caviar, lobster, truffles, Gruyere melted in champagne
steam & Kopi-Luwak-coffee-BBQ sauce you eat on the way to
Tanzania. Have you never lived by a lousy neighbor with a shotgun blazing
ATV down-lawn to taunt the dogs you can't get to come no matter
how you scream? Your 1 child, fevered, to his 3 cans of gasoline burning
chairs at midnight—are you still shopping Sherpa, their shoes rubber-
banded to feet to hump your camp up Kilimanjaro this spring?

He leaves for bootcamp in the morning, but now kegs & loud county-opera
tossing his gal down-street between 2 chickens shot for sport, lit cigarette
she flicks past his head to our weeds while lilacs bloom through
the screen causing grief—I never knew a haute couture existed in the form
of mountain gear, or that prostitutes at your Amsterdam stop come
certified clean & HIV free by the boutique you purchase shrooms to view
Van Goghs once you have peaked, descended, tipped the docent you
mistook for peasant fishing from the 'Langlois Bridge at Arles.'

Do you still bend the ear of your investment broker, life coach, therapist,
& lawyer, the Tarot reader whose specialty is past life regression where
you invariably ride, whether horse or dromedary into the role of
Temujin/Tutankhamen/some king with a problem only your Hatha yogi
can limber you out of, if you catch the private jet to Miami swilling
matcha? Here we have one Sheriff on call, on notice, for arresting citizens
while drunk, best buds with the neighbor's father who somehow sleeps
through his son's bomb-party plus my all-night *Shut the F-ups*.

The gulf between us is a revved truck, whooping morning & my kid wants
cocoa pop pancakes, not grape medicine, Corona-smashed street, the cow
dung entwines muscadine—O smoke gold sunrise in the creek
out back, first trout swim w/jelly-bright eggs still in them, free-throated
geese flock reeds, I spill cheap coffee in the percolator, dress, wave
off the hallucinatory crawdad of no-sleep gnawing fringes of the neighbor's
fresh fatigues—wild to go truffling in the gulf between us for the olive
in the oil, the bridge, the salt to cure this fire kindled thirst

to drink the animals' world.

Wind

Uncle Len keeps coming back from Vietnam stores guns in his basement
to aid an Arkansas Militia won't save him from the fundamentalist series *Left
Behind* has him thinking of the 12-year-old Vietnamese errand runner he gave
cigarettes boy got shot for accepting the gift chain smokes hell is getting coined
Baby Killer when the draft blows doors open if he doesn't accept Jesus into his
heart Nurse Len what if he doesn't want to accept? In his white uniform
stethoscope hands heal patients booby trap Apocalypse likes strawberry jam
all wars don't bleed into one another for everyone what's the part to repent?

Questions spark gold in the gingko's litter the pipeline bolt holds in its mold
& wild horses graze Bahia the steppes of central Asia the graves of our mothers
spring mouths & still lay lakes you can drink from straight—did you know
despite seeming one body of light whole species of lightning bugs fly at differing
heights? Scant elders tend gardens outside the hard drive's census down 9 mile
swamp otter play the architecture of beavers miraculous & today is *so* not
a cloud beautiful you could believe the extinct ivory billed woodpecker still
calls this home calls *come out & play* beside the landfill of defunct cells.

Afternoon Clean

For decades we'd witnessed dark murders
    descend through crop-facing windows—
      so left our eggs un-whisked in batter
        for chase from sheer anger, suds rising, hot
         faucet streams, we forgot our spatulas
          forging to skillets, despite smoke we
           flung coats on, knocked bills akimbo,
            squashed pajamas in galoshes—Christ
            Armageddon—we left our cats crouched
            feral at raw bacon's ledge as we winged
            doors free, fell to knees, field-edge, braced
12 gauges—shot the thieves.

Someone has to clean up the
            shells, toss grease soaked papertowels, lick
          the whisker, soap grass-stained knees,
          sweep fresh tracks, fish the envelope
         spilled down floor vent despite ash &
         throw open the sash, zero out the still-
        flaming gas, trash the molten utensil, hang
       suds-logged rugs, straighten curtains on
      the kitchen Idyll, from sheer obligation—
    re-make morning, scrub the afternoon clean,
  search the crop-facing window—though the
crows were the only things we ever got back.

No Bogeyman Tonight

Then the Popo seemed to declare a secret war on citizens & our cameras caught
them shooting young men in the back & the bus

would leave for even more crazy shit.

& I got educated in the class of Abramović blessing the body Justice—what if,
instead of the donut shop, we all went to church

again, the church of immersion in a stranger's eyes, that is—

& moved by this we grieved unacceptably long—until hair streaked every
window we gazed in, there is no Demon weak as a marksman's

fear.

Walk

The kill was accidental the coyotes did not want the meat the meat
didn't want to be downed that day the rain charged the air
with negative ions we all felt great & walked, garnet crystals flanked
the washed-up creek wind-rush, you know that feeling
of no-surveillance? Curious objects fall—a purple leaf or walnut
in its citron husk, we peeled one bare down to its tannic heart
with 911 a county away, the sky a blank crow caw.

It's not as though the coyotes buttoned up their coyote-suits that
morning plotting to leave a being childless. Whether fowl
or furred the mothers left their hymnals in their caves that day
the same as us—it's not unusual, in fall, to come across
vermillion grasses in the rough part of the fieldpath, but maybe
that's why the coyotes fled the scene so fast: An eerie fear
the meat belonged to family, but which one?

Can it be said that one gets used to either being stalked or stalking?
Having had no recent predators, the coyotes must have felt
free walking the beat—you know that feeling of no-surveillance?
When all the woods are yours to eat, Don't Trespass signs
are landscape. Afterall, we'd been so used to trying not to gain
attention, our sheer movement past the cattails may have startled
the coyotes before the feast, our footsteps sounding

numerous as rain & with winter on fall's heels one might believe
each droplet held an icicle or spectacle for bearing witness
to what pack in nature lay our meat to waste. Rain accents cadmium
vine strung down to chartreuse feather—no lens does justice.
That's why we took the walk, while shivering, & saw this meat
arrested, fresh, & glittering as if to say: Aren't you my kin?

Whoever once walked aimless in these woods now walks awake
with me in death.

Plush

& there were many separations of land from land.

Many mansions' wrought iron fences staked claim on the ground
so adjacent chainlinks seemed fragile nets of mist.

Phonewires wound in clear sight, then went fugitive in vegetation.

Gravel banked our tracks, craters held wet light by the River called
Hudson.

We didn't understand why 2×4s boxed mature trees, PVC joints
flocked mown pasture.

Sometimes a factory, sometimes a park—one angled, the other lay
a concrete runners' arc beside receptacles of trash.

Topiaries made one town cute—another sprung backlots, graffiti
blubbed slabs, spent slugs.

Wherever long rushes went uninterrupted, blue heron dive-bombed
fish or forsythias yellowed slate cliffs.

If the bodies drifting platforms between stations had been unclothed
they would, as we animals, have sloped beautiful in various skins.

In the space between cars, you could stick your arm into wind. That's
where the conductor told

how awful it was for the engineer when the elderly couple parked
their truck against the way of freight—*No way*, he said, *not to look.*

In the river, driftwood, rebar, flag on a pier's end. Having had neither
painter's century, nor genteel brush,

a Space Alien beside us sang kathunk, doowah, shoo. Of what is iron
made? Earth. Of what—the litter & blooms, of what so

what, she uncoupled herself from judgment or use—a watcher
unpained by temporal connection.

> So we searched her bags—
> but found no coin worth purchase.
> So we rent her garments
> & made pretty train
> curtains

> & she didn't seem to care
> we cut her hair—a new material
> for fiddle bows we hoped
> would not give
> out.

Space Alien, I can't reach your origin of spherical & blameless
music fast enough, if it weren't for ocular love,

I do—

Riverdale and Wave Hill were the real names of towns we passed
through. It's eons since we buried mother at the Natural

History Museum & of her face only the essence remains peach
pale pink rose bark bitter shapes shifting dark brown tan gray
wheel going soft flesh the haunted house of the missing
hair pick Someone's banjo riffs unraveled plunked
notes fingers touch blind touch—if you want
Love you will have to batter past Eden
& believe there was no order gar-
den hoe or walleye fish we saw
less felt more no man made
name we no jasmine hold
or celadon jug no ochre
rudder rust root flame
& limitless colorless
hammerless no first
last anvil's fall once
weren't we just

      volume

   plush

full-tilt

  then
     space?

What the engineer couldn'a seen: The old man smelled like the bait shop
that morning. She'd just whispered the most startling, beautiful thing.

Lo Siento, the Only People Who Know Where
Lake Conasauga Is Live There & Aren't Telling

So we three are family, again, with a real job, we move to N.Y., Upstate, journey
to the falls, Chittenango, little soldier booth, $5 entry, we can afford to pay for
the view & lack of riff raff, our fabulous shoes, no holes, beasts tased & carted
elsewhere, so we can't harm them for plundering our wastecan-food—above
the picnic area shitter's sink, signs warn: Don't drink the water, e-coli, farm-
chemical runoff—we never seen such healthy cornfields, sidling up by state
park, saint park, we walk through the so called woods, to the silvery falls, arrows
every 5 yards point the way so we can't get lost, even if we want, plus it's a just
a sinewy pig path flanked by an 8 ft. chainlink with more signs posted to that:
Don't smoke, litter, or feed the wildlife, & watch them, your children, don't jump,
don't dive/swim, so we can't wholly picture them—the leaves & falls—it's just us
& our single-filing-family monk-feet, packing down wrapper-free dirt behind
Marmot-draped tourists, one with a kid struggling against her leash, she wants
to see what's beyond us—at the pinnacle, a sign signifies a boulder, like we don't
know one, which it's more a couch, anyway, where to pose for the ideal picture's
marked with more arrows—we get the idea, we slip front or back of that spot?
Ranger's going to frisk us, which popo-types do downstate, anyway, if they want
to, if they got suspicion of a gun, which even though we aren't packing—we do
look it, guilty of something, not like the 75+ Amish who barefoot a ball in their
hats & hairthings, fieldside of the parking lot where, once you have your money's
worth of pristine, you can drive back, changed-good for not touching anything,
anything in nature—we better behave.

Y'all haven't always tried to, behave. Before this journey, the so called free
home-wrecker weekend, no fence between couples, you smoked your chemical
runoff, corn-whiskey-highball hitting wood floor, wood splintering into a wildpig
forest you call Conasauga, in the mythical lore of Georgia, you spiraled up, then
down again, looking for the state park, devil park, three times, no signs, wheels
flung rocks down twin ravines either side of midnight, headlights struck red
eyes of god knows what flesh-starved wildcat, & between death journeys, you
asked directions in the valley below's 24-hour Circle K, where the clerk said *Lo
siento*, it didn't exist, this place, you fed the wildlife: Pizza flavored Combos, pork
rinds, Twinkies, Cokes, anything denying health existed, you avid hawk, you
bullfrog unbelting in the babyclothes closet with Fang, trees looking the same,

it all reminded you, once you found the mountain sites by accident, by animal instinct, unrangered, unmown—of the downhome whiteboy gangbang, Juliana & Lollie with their throats slit in the Appalachian Trail tent, a decade hence, lawless chicory-fragrance, Dickey's fabulous sex-slaughters, twang & shotgun blast, wreckage of fern-ripped, A.T.V.s droned in the close-by, muckstink of morning, bugs buzzed like struck matches, it felt good, at the time, though, unfettered marsh lark, the took permission to touch rare wildflowers in that neglected chain of foothills—the baby alone, asleep, in the next room's manger, Muddy Waters, loud, played, while next year's ghost shat between trees—O ruiner of holy things, orange butterflies flared out from a lightning struck stump, you the lightning, rift & decay, brushing fire ants off your face.

Weirdly, down from Chittenango a ways, we took our boy, Hallows Eve or All Saint's Day, to a haunted corn maze, cider, organic pumpkin seeds, kids dressed as princesses & killers from various films. The dusk hayride proved convincing, if more terror-struck than expected, the wagon's jerk & reeling over frost crusted dry humps in the fieldpath, fog ghosted pond scum, figures hung & swinging in the wind-torched trees, they wore orange jumpsuits, their faces a deep shade of stuffed pantyhose—we paid to take the hayride twice, for confirmation we saw the lynching we seen, this far North, this millennium, yesterday, we did!—but kept it from our son, little Zeus, little Arab-Jew, still, it made sense, Chittenango, wanting physical signs to point the way out—so the next trip, we went to *Aida*, laptops in this version of Egypt, every opera singer belting out Italian was walnut, persimmon, birch, or ash-tongued, we didn't understand a word of it, but connected, viscerally.

Weirdly, the third night at Conasauga, a white truck circled your tent, so haunted you locked yourself in your car—but with no keys to move it, you tried ducking under the dash, too fat, the muscle-necked, shotgun-toting devil fenced in your jalopy & approached, anyway, through dusky, rain whelped trees, no husband, no child—you felt alone in the place you thought you couldn't recover from the apocalyptic past or present, yours, or that of others, & beside the brute stalked a spit-slinging pitbull, off-leash—you made the rash decision to open your door & meet death—but the man said he was just Roger, hunting wild boar he donated to the local meat locker, for the poor, which you used to be, when you ate squirrel, one pig could save a family of twelve from starving, Roger said & all the firewood lay soaked with the afternoon torrents, so Roger sped down dirt & brought you back two dry truckfulls, he refused your beer & left—but built you a big, warm fire, before vanishing.

I get so turned around sometimes, poor then lame, broken then rich enough to own sneakers nobody but me has ever tried on, or worn—wild then fixed, I don't know where, or who I am, or was, will be, or between you & me, if there's any difference, woods being so various—what's your sign? Mine's the Starfish, located at the crossroads where the Southern Cross/Polaris meet & I'm amazed by you—your brand new limbs.

Upon Pouring Tabasco on the Variegated Thyme to Save it from the Chipmunk

We were, each of us, sure how the world should go:
Blue jay dive-bombed squirrel for seed—
over neighboring fields, storm clouds rolled low
& porcine deer clipped our tulips to knees—
yet the deer-deterrent we sprayed smelled so gross
we couldn't breathe the outdoors for weeks,
then the cowbird dumped her egg in wren's home—
do katydids record a score for *Creep?*
Over neighboring fields, not ours, clouds rolled,
the dog's mouth caught corn snake's shadow,
the rumor proliferate: Cell waves slay bees—
we were, each of us, sure how the world should go:
While moths favored many discreet black holes,
the televangelists agreed on brimstone
& over neighboring fields, stone clouds rolled low
yet rain held drink from drought fires in limbo,
so we let our garden go to thistle-weeds
while machetes came in vogue on murder-TV,
we were, each of us, sure how the world should go—
against dark clouds, fields' gorgeous gloam.

ACKNOWLEDGMENTS

Grateful acknowledgments are due to the editors of the following literary magazines and online publications where these poems (some with alternate titles and versions) first appeared:

The Birmingham Review, 25th Anniversary Issue: "Wha Wha Pedal" and "Afternoon Clean" (*Best American Poetry, 2014*); *Corresponding Voices:* "On Finding the Lost Scissors," "Stranger's Song," "The Ghost, the Driver, the Martyr," "The Rock," and "Wind,"; *Hazlitt:* "Moth"; *Lo-Ball:* "We Could Not Get Lost"; *Plume:* "Woo," "Plush," "Paper," "Pink," "Velvetleaf," and "Calling Home"; *Smartish Pace:* "Upon Pouring Tabasco on the Variegated Thyme to Save it From the Chipmunk"; "*The Progressive:* "Gulf"; *The Southern Review:* "Lilacs," "Winter Reading," and "Walk" (*Pushcart, 2017*).

Walk Till the Dogs Get Mean: Meditations on the Forbidden from Contemporary Appalachia: "Lo Siento, the Only People Who Know Where Lake Conasauga Is Live There & Aren't Telling."

& to the Whiting Foundation & the National Endowment for the Arts
& to The MacDowell Colony, for their generous fellowship & community of
    writers
& to Hamilton College, for providing the Kirkland Fellowship
& to David Smith, MaryKatherine Callaway, Neal Novak (what wondrous editing), and all those at LSU Press
& to dear friends Jules Gibbs, Naomi Guttman, James Kimbrell, and Bruce
    Smith, who helped me shape this book

& to the family, all—but especially John and Morrison.

CPSIA information can be obtained
at www.ICGtesting.com
Printed in the USA
LVHW09s1428230818
587897LV00002B/282/P

9 780807 167922